Lee Castle

A Poetic Tour

Poetry, illustrations and photographs

by Malcolm Buller

With additional material by Andrew Buller

Published by Andrew Buller Books - www.andrewbuller.co.uk

First published in Great Britain in 2021 - Text and illustration copyright © 2021 Malcolm Buller

I am greatly indebted to Andrew Buller for sharing his expertise to produce this book.

I acknowledge that the cover photograph and those on pages 118 and 147 come from Canva Pro.

All rights reserved. No part of this publication may be reproduced, stored in a retrieval system, or transmitted, in any form or by any means, electronic, mechanical, photocopying, recording or otherwise, without the prior permission of the copyright owner.

Also by Malcolm Buller

What's in the box? A poetical miscellany

Parallel Lies – a novel set in 1960s London

For further information about my work
and that of my publisher please go to
Andrew Buller's website
www.andrewbuller.co.uk

For further poetry try
Corona Linings – Prophetic Rhymings
by Andrew Buller

Acknowledgements

I acknowledge the help given by our son, Andrew,
in the encouragement to write and illustrate, but also for
his expertise in the production of this book.

The patience of my wife, Joan, has also been stretched,
both during our visits and whilst the muse is with me.

We also thank the staff of Leeds Castle for their helpful
and cheerful manners which does so much to make
everyone welcome.

She

She sits silently

serene

in full view of all

confident of her position

the centre of attention

yet aloof

untouchable.

Dressed in cream

her subtle shapes portray strength beneath the beauty.

She's placed herself right at the water's edge

dangling as a precipice

reflecting her glory in double image.

As the soft white clouds part

sunlight sparkles gold upon her form

casting shadows

emphasising contours

which tantalise

the envious eyes

of those who stand and stare

hypnotised by the unobtainable.

She knows

they think

she is

the loveliest in the world.

Introduction

'Leeds Castle – A Poetic Tour' takes you on a journey around what has been described as 'the loveliest castle in the world'.

It was in December 2019 that, with my wife, I first came to Leeds. We are fortunate to live just a few miles away so planned to be able to visit during the different seasons of the year. The months that followed affected everyone, everything and everywhere, so we were very grateful, once allowed, to have such beautiful surroundings in which to take regular exercise.

At first, whilst Joan enjoyed observing the bird life,
I took snapshots hoping to capture the changing
scenes. As our pace of life changed, I found myself
drawn to put words to what I saw. As poetry
emerged, so did aspects of the castle and grounds
that I had previously passed by.

Use this guide as you will. It might be a souvenir
of your only visit or a trail of exploration, a snapshot
of a day or a pointer to further treasures to explore.

The weather, people, events, history and nature are
ever-changing subjects for the 'have-a-go' poet,
yet here also we can find such variety of peace and
activity. The water flows ever down, yet lies so still,
watched over by the majesty of this royal castle,
'the loveliest in the world'.

Malcolm Buller
September 2021

The author

Malcolm and his wife, Joan, live in rural Kent where they are fully immersed in village life. They are retired primary school teachers.

Malcolm often wrote alongside his pupils, tackling their task and sharing the results. Many pupils found their work came alive when read aloud. He encouraged all to follow where the subject took them, yet also have a surprise ending as a possibility. Displaying work by the whole class on the wall or in a book added to the status of the writing. Such books often became a favourite choice to borrow from the class library.

The Poetic Tour

The letters on the sketch map that follows relate to the poems located in that area. They have been inspired by observations or happenings at or near these places within the castle estate. The route is greatly influenced by the one-way system instigated during the early 2020s. Put together they form a tour, or perhaps more importantly, act as a stimulus for the visitor to put pen to paper as another 'Have-a-go' poet.

If you are inspired to write, then please do.
Send your thoughts to mpbuller1@btinternet.com.
With enough interest, a second volume based on contributions could ensue. All contributors would be suitably acknowledged and kept informed of publication details.

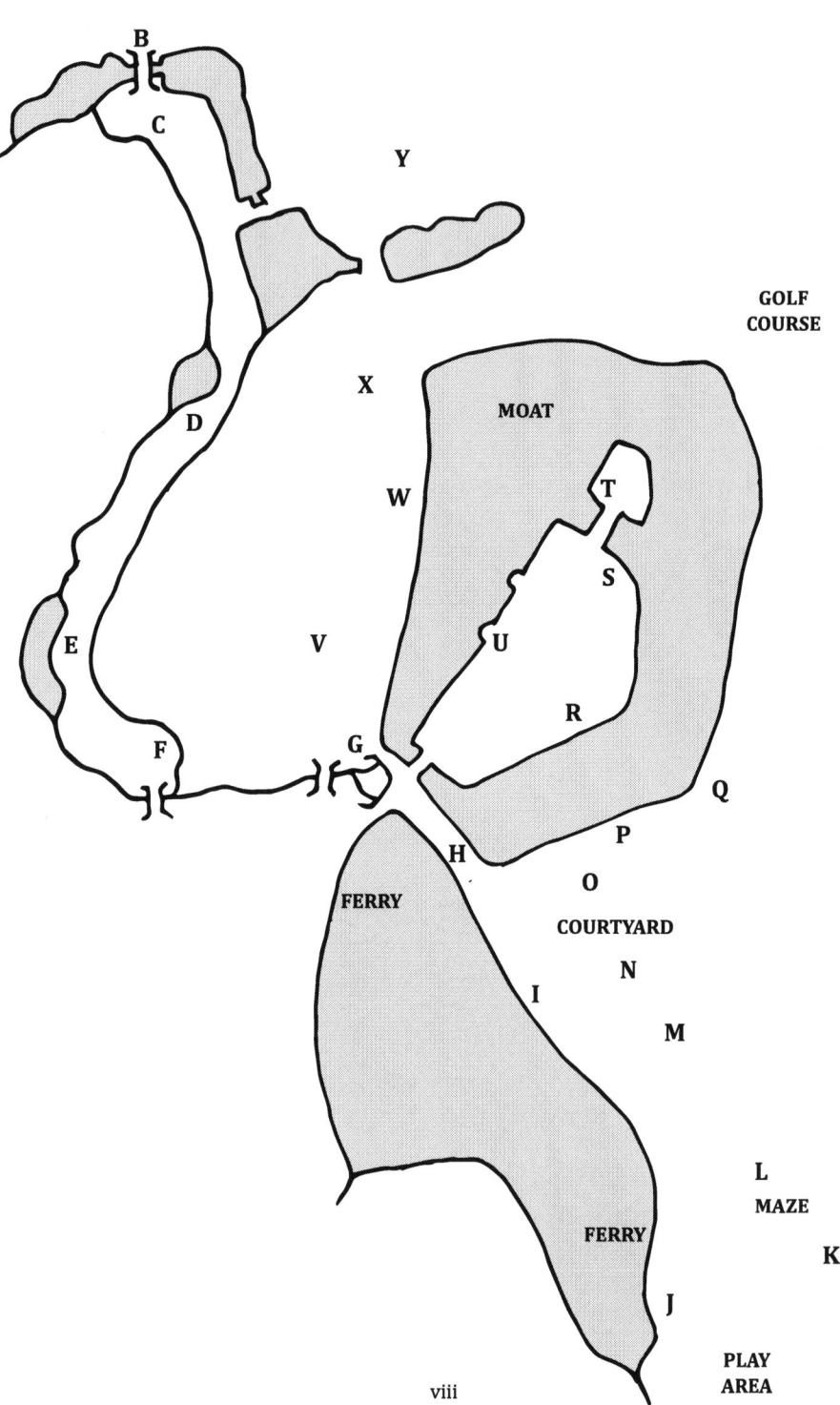

Leeds Castle - A Poetic Tour

A	Pause awhile	1
B	Bridge over rippled water	5
C	Take care	9
D	Grey fish	17
E	Ode to the willow	19
F	Trees	31
G	The old mill	39
H	What secrets lie inside?	41
I	In days gone by the birds fly free	43
J	Growth	50
K	Challenge	55
L	A maze	57
M	The formal gardens	63
N	A dog's life	67
O	Castle wed	69
P	Reflect on this	71
Q	A rocky outcrop	73
R	Come walk with me	82
S	I have feelings	83
T	Pax vobiscum	91
U	Timepiece	98
V	Let's face it	102
W	In its waters	103
X	To sit and stare	105
Y	Plantation	107
Z	Grandmother's treat	108

Contents

	Page	Tour Stop
Acknowledgements	i	
She	ii	
Introduction	iv	
The author	vi	
The Poetic Tour	vii	
Sketch map	viii	
Contents	x	
Pause awhile	1	A
History marches on	3	
Bridge over rippled water	5	B
Finding peace	7	
Battle lines	8	
Take care	9	C
The waterfall	11	
Segway daze	13	
Grass grows	14	
Doubt	15	
Conflict	16	
Grey fish	17	D
Ode to the willow	19	E

	Page	Tour Stop
Weeping willows	23	
The ballad of the gunnera	27	
Trees	31	F
Brief encounter	33	
Ducklings	34	
Visitors	35	
The old mill	39	G
What secrets lie inside?	41	H
In days gone by the birds fly free	43	I
Black swan	45	
White feather	47	
Mouldiwarp	49	
Growth	50	J
I'm the King of the Castle	51	
Crazy golf	52	
Challenge	55	K
Eagle eyes	56	
A maze	57	L
Typheous	61	
The formal gardens	63	M
Proud	64	

	Page	Tour Stop
Random thoughts	65	
A dog's life	67	N
Castle wed	69	O
The eye of the beholder	70	
Reflect on this	71	P
A rocky outcrop	73	Q
Playing around	75	
Where sound Leeds	77	
The causeway leads	79	
Come walk with me	82	R
I have feelings	83	S
Upon the stair	85	
Rights	86	
Queen's gallery	87	
The Queen's maidens	88	
The dragon flies	89	
Pax vobiscum	91	T
May 22nd 1520	93	
Twist	94	
Cool warmth	95	
Lady Baillie	97	
Timepiece	98	U
The new castle	99	

	Page	Tour Stop
The Maiden's Tower	101	
Let's face it	102	V
In its waters	103	W
To sit and stare	105	X
Plantation	107	Y
Grandmother's treat	108	Z
A slant on history	**109**	
Early days	110	
The ballad of Eleanor	115	
The young queens	119	
The seasons	**122**	
A royal spring	123	
"Let mists arise!"	125	
It's hot!	126	
The leaves are turning	129	
The English autumn	131	
Foggy Leeds	133	
Christmas trees	134	
Winter colours	135	
Years to remember	**137**	
Released from lockdown's grip	138	
Set benchmarks high	142	
Golfers' roundelay	143	

Pause awhile

The semi-circular seat suggests we sit

– yet few do.

The hellebores in bloom have bowed their heads

– so I do too

listening for robin's contact call,

skulking amongst camellias or perched on boughs

proclaiming presence to all rivals

– old or new.

Footsteps running, pushchair wheels in hot pursuit

– sharp words ensue.

Snatched conversation snippets, walking frames

– path width for two.

Yet from this seat I picture worlds passed by,

imagination's eyes see zig-zag bridge,

reflections, willow tears refreshing waterfowl,

glimpse future delights upon the road ahead

– my true blue view.

History marches on

A bar of metal orders, "Halt!"

A date – a message clear for all –

stone castle built

nine centuries since.

"Quick march!"

Left, right,

up and down

we marvel at our present space

until we reach another date

with history.

"Mark time!"

A gloriette

built for a queen

called Eleanor.

Our wandering pathway

leads us through

a royal siege

imprisonment

a battlefield

or meeting place.

"Stand at – ease!"

Admire

the many wonders

time has wrought

on its journey to today.

"Stand easy."

Bridge over rippled water

The birds will congregate to greet each child

armed with paper bags of seeds to sow

delight or envy in the feathered ranks

as spills on land or slip to those below

who paddle hard against the water's power

as all lake's contents funnelled, narrowed, flow

across the concrete channel under wood

to re-emerge to help the weeds to grow.

Yet seeds have sprouted more than verdant fronds

as glinting circles catch each of sun's rays

from passing lovers' coins that held a wish

and for a change became their throwaways.

The restless stream moves all towards the drop,

the tipping point, life's balance here outweighs

the turbulence of money-grabbing greed

and helps preserve the best of waterways.

Finding peace

If your travelling has been stressful

    walk peacefully Leeds Castle grounds.

    When with traffic noise your head pounds

and your whole day's been eventful –

reward – admire the beautiful –

    natural and built inside these bounds.

If your travelling has been stressful

    walk peacefully Leeds Castle grounds.

Savour clean fresh air so restful –

    listen to breeze and birdsong sounds –

take memories away, non-fretful,

if your travelling has been stressful

    walk peacefully Leeds Castle grounds.

Battle lines

Cuprous eagle sits
orientally aloof
in all weathers, vain.

His turning gaze lights
upon the foe, curled quite still,
ready, unblinking.

Battle scars abound
for talons tear, teeth and jaws
return searing fire.

Aloft her tree trunk
dragon only bides her time,
awaits whistling winds.

These angry adversaries
pose their threats, but carry none.

A Haiku Sonnet

Take care

Now when you walk this path you must take care
As something's watching you from a great height.
Mind all the creatures – don't cause them to fright –
Each needs to live securely in their lair.

Tiptoe past the shrubbery – if you dare –
Hold safe a hand – ensure your eyes are bright –
Expect surprise – and maybe say a prayer.

Dark and brooding – curled up aloft – don't stare –
Ready to roar and set the world alight –
Always alert with monstrous teeth to bite –
Grasping her victims – wriggling in despair.
Oh – how can we tame this fearsome dragon?
Name her – be friendly – call her Aragon!

Acrostic rhymes use the first letter of each line to spell out a name or message.

The waterfall

The yellow-bellied grey wagtail

his cousin pied he vies for flies

amidst the spray and constant flow

of waterfall.

Above, the mighty cedars stand

though far from home in Lebanon

refreshed and nurtured constantly

by waterfall.

Each year rings true, for deep inside,

each season marked at its demise

the sap will rise again sustained

through waterfall.

So stand and marvel at the scene

from tiny insect, glorious tree

all owe existence here to one

great waterfall.

Segway daze

Above the waterfall a causeway path
invites the visitor to stop and gaze,
yet care is needed not to take a bath

especially if Segway paid-for days
finds you atop a powered set of wheels
where forwards and reverse leave you in haze.

Ignore your comrades' suicidal squeals
and focus how your leader beckons you.
You know that falls can hurt, but blood congeals
and you have made it back, in safety, phew!

Grass grows

The grass greenly grows,

the mower rhythmically mows,

but suddenly a shudder and shake

avoiding action you must take

as from the earth

witness rebirth

the dead decaying trunk

with clink and clunk

comes back to life –

carved as if by knife –

chainsaw chipped –

no longer nondescript.

What form did this art take?
A gentle benign snake.

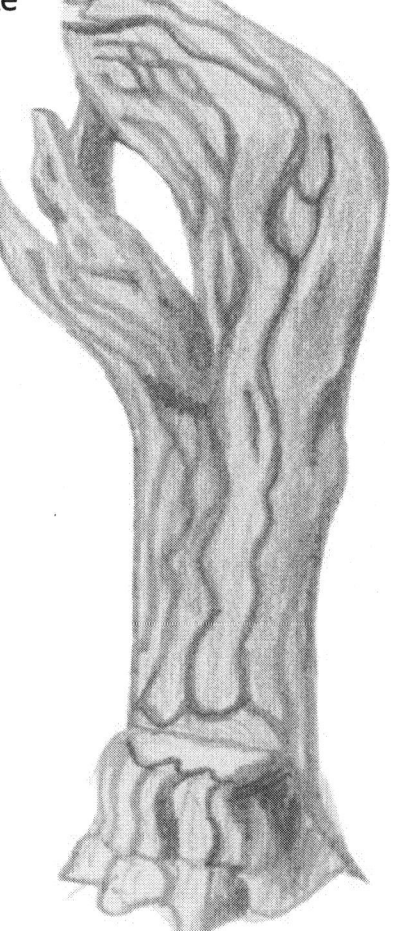

Doubt

From dense mist fingers beckon

twisting their message

to follow – or flee?

Sinews strain to gather attention

furrows spattered

thickening arms outstretched

offering doubt –

sanctuary or captivity?

Conflict

Grey fish swims safely

in the knowledge of his life

beneath lake's surface

    watching his mirror

    on the world above, beyond

    imagination.

Grey heron paddles,

both feet in fish's realm, but

mind is crystal clear,

    stillness is the key,

    breathe, until the time is right,

    patiently wait.

A flash of conscience?

One of life's lessons.

Grey fish

Grey fish glides effortlessly along
the edges of the lake
surveying his mirror-world close-to.

A tiny moorhen chick breaks cover
away from gaping jaws
and plunges deep into the reeds.

The thresholds warm to the morning rays
slowing his rhythmic tail
and calling others into his kingdom.

The shallows welcome schools
to learn to feed
and prosper here under his tutelage.

The plants sprout strong and straight
towards the shining lights
aloft in that reversed image.

That grey image, statuesque,
with shining eyes
and steel-sharpened bill

that spears through fears
and plucks another helping
through the looking-glass of life.

Ode to the willow

O all-embracing willow tree,

your strength's displayed for all to see

rooted secure within the passing brook,

holding fast, yet gently, like a shepherd's crook

cradles the lamb, struggling for breath

in watery torrent, near death,

but you give life and comfort to us all,

protecting us from floods when waters fall

from heaven's anger. You hold fast banks,

drink your fill, with our grateful thanks.

Your mighty trunk can twist and turn

as nature dictates. We all learn

how early spring will catkins hang your boughs

and slender thongs cascading that allows

ravenous insects dance their dance
to pollinate your neighbour, entrance
aphids, their sweet honeydew entice ants
in turn fall prey to birds. You giant plants
are the life-givers to this land,
without – no single thing could stand.

As summer's sun beats down, your shade,
dappled, cooling, great shelter made
for snoozing mallards, within their waddle
escape to dive, refreshed, perfect idyll
for courting couples, hidden vows
beneath your whispering, secret boughs
true love was pledged, throughout your age-long life
and some, maybe, became husband and wife,
but even so – you aren't to blame.
O great Willow – we praise your name.

You are so valuable. Great use

man's artful mind has sought, deduce

to fashion string, his fishing nets, bats, boats,

fences, handles and paper for his notes

on how his ailments that abound,

cures for fever willow sap found

how acetylsalicylic acid,

now called aspirin, cures. So, for all did

our esteemed Willow this tribute raise.

We do not weep for thee – we praise!

Weeping willows

What will the darting wagtail wish
beside the streams? No, not the fish,
but insects, spiders, juicy flies
where weeping willows whisper wise.

The heron stalks throughout the day
yes focused, sharp, to hypnotise
a passing eel, or fish, his prey
where weeping willows whisper wise.

The peacock struts, head held aloof,
and chases mate upon the roof –
so rarely hides, or loudly cries –
where weeping willows whisper wise.

The female mallard and her drake
all thoughts of fear seem to despise.
The shortest route to food they'll take
where weeping willows whisper wise.

The dabchick dives beneath the scene,
a little grebe, but he survives
through underwater speed, serene
where weeping willows whisper wise.

The buzzard's master of the skies –
the thermal draft he'll upward take
above reflection in the lake
where weeping willows whisper wise.

Now stately swans, whooper and black,

along with mute, their foes attack –

then preen – and feed – and close their eyes –

where weeping willows whisper wise.

Wandering water hides surprise

where weeping willows whisper wise.

I wonder – when, who, which – and whys

where weeping willows whisper wise.

The ballad of the gunnera

All winter long he lies in wait

for victims to come near –

a drab old lump in lifeless state,

ignored, devoid of fear.

Perhaps a spider may perchance

to spin a net for flies

and thrill to feel their frantic dance

as trapped they are like spies.

As spring's impulses flow again

the gunnera breaks free

it's armoury, a spiky mane

on stems for all to see.

As leaves unfurl they too are blessed
with spears so caution's needed.
Blaspheming words escape the chest
if this advice ain't headed.

The summer sun brings growth apace
and gunnera are racing
to fight each other up to space –
it's so exhilarating.

The tallest welcomes humans in
to stand beneath its brolly,
sheltering from the raindrops din
whilst yaffle laughs at folly.

So take your photos with great care,

no close-ups if you're wise

as autumn breezes often dare

to spring a sharp surprise.

The gunnera is waiting still

his army grows each year

so tiptoe by, ignore his quill,

stick on the path that's clear.

Trees

Admiring beauty of the trees,

wonder why or how they grew

here by chance, planted with stories.

Birds brought seeds, pollinating bees,

teeming life abounds for you

admiring beauty of the trees.

Sources of food, nuts and berries,

dappled lighting frames the view

here by chance, planted with stories.

How seed produced two chimneys,

mystery unsolved, but true,

admiring beauty of the trees.

Honour these abnormalities,

just walk by or climb on through,

Here by chance, planted with stories

of broken hearts, elves and fairies,

kiddies playing peek-a-boo,

admiring beauty of the trees,

here by chance, planted with stories.

Brief encounter

river divided

doubles opportunities

kingfisher plunges

turquoise

sheen

waterproof

plumage

The nature themes of the well-known Haiku poetic form have been adapted to a modern Hanku, made from just four words.

Ducklings

I freely wander round Leeds Castle grounds

where baby ducklings always make me smile.

    Just watch them waddle up in single file

        whilst mother makes maternal worried sounds.

        They'll hide and seek amongst leafy surrounds

        and tease my eyes to pause and stare awhile.

I freely wander round Leeds Castle grounds

where baby ducklings always make me smile.

    Ducklings' antics entertain and astounds

        the little child as each dropped seed or pile

        disappears like magic. Their simple guile,

        outdo siblings, as seen on children's playgrounds.

I freely wander round Leeds Castle grounds

where baby ducklings always make me smile.

Visitors

One strides the paths with walking poles

intent on progress

barely taking time to glance

at fish or bird or plant or stream.

He is alone in conversation

of just where he might have been

without appreciation.

    The pensioners seek out the resting places

    and watch the world go by.

    Time to savour sights and sounds,

    react to every passing breeze

    and grasp the beauty

    in reflection of the trees.

The camera lens is long.

Her model knows the pose

the angles to adopt.

The castle captured

lured by maiden's charms

and yet as turn their backs on beauty

the clouds depart

and sunlight adds such intimacy.

    Children have one goal in mind

    furthest point to climb and chase

    pretend to fight

    explore relationships with strangers

    finding who might be a loyal friend

    or fiendish foe.

    Promises of ice cream treats

    agree it's time to go.

The twitcher scans the lake for rarities.

Grey wagtails

statuesque

on edge-stones ridge

flick tails

and dash to rid the world of midge.

    The dabchick too breaks surface

    gulps in breath and dives again

    almost missed

    leaving just an ever-growing ripple

    and a tick upon her list.

Buggy-pushing mothers chatter

as their boys disappear

through the gate that opens

accessing a grassy slope

towards cascading weir.

    Ex-teachers exchange

    understanding words

    their smiles are hard to mask

    and leave the parents

    to their unenviable task.

The poet savours all

hoping thoughts and words

will later take their moment to enthral.

The old mill

The old mill feels all astride the water
since centuries gone by. The river slow.
The castle's role – controlling pressure.

    "Dam and channel – harness power!"
    "Grind the corn our farmers grow!"
    The old mill feels all astride the water.

"Defend our assets – another structure!"
"A barbican will check the flow!"
The castle's role – controlling pressure.

    The lakes are formed – sluice gates the feeder –
    direct the energy below.
    The old mill feels all astride the water.

Thousands fed through this mill's flour –

but time takes toll – decay will follow.

The castle's role – controlling pressure.

    A picturesque scene – gushing like thunder –

    for all to wonder – today – tomorrow.

        The old mill feels all astride the water.

        The castle's role – controlling pressure.

What secrets lie inside?

What secrets lie inside these islands fair?
A mirrored finish – smooth as polished glass.
No warnings given – suspense in the air
creeps stealthily where no man dares to pass.

Seen from distance, through history's spyglass,
successive owners made their mark, declare
enemies must this castle here bypass.
What secrets lie inside these islands fair?

Are jilted lovers from a doomed affair
or suitors for a maid beyond their class
lying below tranquil moat in despair?
A mirrored finish – smooth as polished glass.

A glint of metal, steel or solid brass,
an oaken door, thick sandstone walls take care
of all who venture near. 'Do not trespass' –
no warnings given – suspense in the air.

Wanderers marvel – stand awhile and stare –

or sit and eat a picnic on the grass –

whilst shadow – cloaked in mystery – with flair –

creeps stealthily where no man dares to pass.

                    What secrets lie inside?

In days gone by the birds fly free

In days gone by – exotic birds were here –

much-loved, admired, their plumage caught the eye –

or maybe call and song assailed your ear –

     in days gone by.

The collection brought in crowds who watched birds try

to reach in vain the air that's blue and clear,

but stayed constrained within their cage to fly.

Perhaps some hid in shrubbery in fear –

forlorn, resigned to never reach the sky –

and yet, perhaps, some people shed a tear –

     in days gone by.

The birds fly free – this tranquil lakeside place

gives safety in this garden sanctuary

where fledglings learn to hide – escape the chase –

     the birds fly free.

A toucan sundial plaque is here to see

the shadow passing slowly o'er its trace

remembers days gone by – and so can we.

But now exotic plants thrive here – they grace

these terraces with blooms to tempt each bee

and benches too where sunlight warms each face –

    the birds fly free!

Black swan

The black swan sails serenely on the lake

beside its mate. The mallard too with drake

dabbles near water's edge, rise to land

on grassy bank where lovers, hand-in-hand,

are camped, using the natural windbreak.

The courting couple rise, the dust they shake

from clothes, admire the cacti, breath intake

and see the ferry boat from their grandstand.
    The black swan sails.

The engine's throb makes passengers all quake

and black swans rise and fall upon the wake.

On every voyage by the old deckhand

excited children asked to sit, not stand

as waves to land could be a grave mistake.

    The black swan sails.

White feather

I look to heaven and wonder whether

I see aloft a downy snowy flake,

drifting silently. The pure white feather

of fragility, hexagonal frost-

fashioned perfection. Deepest breath intake,

I look to heaven and wonder whether

it can be all alone, seemingly lost

in this warm wilderness, here by mistake,

drifting silently. The pure white feather

caught in eddying breeze, buffeted, tossed
amongst the willow trees edging the lake,
I look to heaven and wonder whether

it's gone forever. My soul counts the cost
until my eye espies, cure for heartache,
drifting silently, the pure white feather

floats ever downwards, and lands, fingers crossed,
in my palm. Soft swan's down, senses awake,
I look to heaven and wonder. Whither
drift on, silently, my pure white feather?

Mouldiwarp

The finest castle builder in the land

I keep my shovels sharp upon each hand.

All day I swim the breaststroke underground

exploring routes, escape and food I've found.

I live alone – a solitary life –

until time comes to find myself a wife.

I dig her nest beneath a fortress mound

and give her the best earthworms that I've found.

Mouldiwarp comes from the Olde English 'molde' meaning earth and 'werpen' to throw. Mouldiwarp is a dialect name for the mammal whose presence can be seen in molehills.

Growth

Thrust from the dust where ashes fell from yesteryear
speared shafts emerge through crusty dirt devoid of fear,
gathering moisture, nutrients and precious light
to gain their precedence, winning battle's fight
against all rivals, ever upwards, pushing out
lime green shoots, inhabiting each space, seem to shout,
"Look, but do not touch!" The clustered stems stretch wide
providing shelter, safety, perfect place to hide
for insects, birds and creatures of the darkest night.
But welcome warmth of summer sun with fierce daylight
provokes response, chemical change which splits the skin
revealing life's true character from deep within.
Whispering grasses daintily dancing assumes
victory for feathered fragility of pampas plumes.

I'm the King of the Castle

adventure	running	attacking	stronghold
exploration	excitement	knights	safety
wonder	courtyard	imagination	peaceful
squires	defences	warfare	playground

The modern Hanku has been squared. It's fun to play up, down, across and diagonally!

Crazy Golf

We paid the price, are given club and ball
and entering the pitch, find number one.
I look and judge the distance, how to stand –
a pendulum, a clunk, eye on the putt
as ball decides direction it's off to
perimeter of green – away from hole.

Another three before it finds its hole.
Opponent down in less. With better ball
he will now show the way to flagpole two.
Up mountain slope to gutter in just one
where gravity delivers simple putt.
Five times I try to reach – alone I stand.

Each numbered flag entices us to stand
devising route to take towards its hole.
Direct across the causeway goes his putt
whilst in the moat the journey for my ball.
This model castle certainly has won
as I am tempted club to break in two.

Great rocky islands bar our journey too –
angles of ricochet I understand –
and bounce from rock could cause a hole-in-one –
I can but dream. With practice on the whole,
I see improvement. Control of the ball
as it leaves the club enhances each putt.

Past grotesque figures flies each uphill putt
seeking its goal as if it knows whereto
it's behind. Too hard – and off it flies – I bawl,

"Fore!" Thank goodness. We learn where's safe to stand —
probably best here — in front of the hole.
Each challenge is quite a different one.

This next looks impossible — no bridge. One
must fly the water jump with a hard putt.
Deep breath — swing — strike — it flies into the hole!
Disbelief. My rival takes a bath — too
bad — I'm sure my joy he'll understand.
Too soon we've reached the last. I aim my ball.

Finding its one goal it shoots aloft. "Two!"
My putt is true. I stand and watch. He strikes.
Up chute to hole. What fun! Where's crazy ball gone?

The Sestina can seem a crazy poetic form, yet it is governed by a strict pattern for its lines, as well as its use of homonyms or repeated rhymes.

Challenge

The old owl

sits still and stares

at the wide world.

The young child

stands still and stares

at the old owl.

Who will blink first?

Who will utter a sound?

Who has the control

to remain motionless?

One

has flown away

defeated.

Eagle eyes

Perched high on tree tops

or castle towers

the hawk waits patiently

assessing victim's options of escape

from plummeting talons' grasp.

> The flying falcon dominates
>
> all speeding records
>
> turns and swoops again
>
> streamlined and graceful in its flight
>
> a seagull look-alike.

Exception

is the silent swooping owl

whose feathers filter out the sound

hearing distant heartbeats

to procure its meal.

A maze

The time has come. Enter the maze.
Follow the pathway of delight
until the parting of the ways.
This way – that way – go left – that's right.

The hedges climb and end in bays
which limits vision, cuts out light.
"Reverse direction," father says,
"this way – that way – go left – that's right."

'Some children disappear for days,'
mother worries when out of sight
her brood escape her beady gaze
this way – that way – go left – that's right.

Before too long she stops and prays.
Then one jumps out to "Boo!" a fright.
She grabs her hand – that's one who stays –
this way – that way – go left – that's right.

She listens hard – mind in a haze –
for voices echoing through the site.
There's no-one near to help liaise –
this way – that way – go left – that's right.

Calmness now – clear-thinking pays
dividends – help to solve her plight –
with tighter curves and sunlight's rays
this way – that way – go left – that's right.

A rocky outcrop then displays

above the hedgerow's towering height.

Her renewed energy she plays

this way – that way – go left – that's right.

They climb the steps in grateful praise

and find their smiles have come alight

for far away – they spot their preys –

this way – that way – go left – that's right.

Eventually, with long delays,

the boys drag father there in spite

of his directions – in a daze,

"This way – that way – go left – that's right."

The moral of this tale we raise.

It's wisdom for some males – we might

suggest – listen to mother when she says,

"This way – that way – go left." – She's right.

Typheous

Do you know Typheous? Don't know?

You have been to Leeds where most go

      to the heart of the maze – where – phew –

      at last escape comes into view –

through the bowels of the grotto.

Typheous sought to overthrow

the Gods of Heaven. Zeus was so

      angered, he – if Greek myths are true –

      dispatched him to his barbecue

in Tartaros – on fire below.

      You do know Typheous.

Typheous rages – eyes aglow –

beneath earth's crust – a volcano

of raging gales and molten spew –

he feels release long overdue –

from torment in this inferno.

Now you know Typheous!

The formal gardens

The formal gardens bloom throughout the year

so sit awhile and ponder at your ease.

The robin perched on hedge –

the wren who loudly sings –

the peacock strutting by will show no fear.

He is the master now of all he sees.

The roses in their beds are nurtured here

by gardeners who pray upon their knees,

"Forgive my sharpened edge."

The deepest cut still stings

as 'Anne Boleyn' is executed, tear

drops, dead-headed, fragrant in the breeze.

Proud

A feathered friend

struts his stuff

ensured of rapt attention

from both young and old.

From startling crown

electric gown

down

through mottled wings

to extravagance of tails

he has it all.

Proud as a peacock.

Random thoughts

It's been a tiring day.

Overnight showers

produce very muddy puddles

you love to explore

in red wellies.

The Squires Courtyard

ran me off my feet

searching for my errant knight.

What a picnic

you devoured.

And now the long walk

your energy has sapped.

Box hedges

clipped in cubes

the yews too

are smartly dressed

so why aren't you?

A mini-maze of paths

through flower beds

lead to the dogs.

Which would fit you best?

What's that?

Come again

tomorrow.

I can't.

Why?

Because .....

it's Daddy's turn.

A dog's life

Do you get hot under the collar?

Are you often sent to bed?

Are you kept on a tight leash

or are you easily led?

Do you feel you're in the dog house

for some things you might have said?

Perhaps that's a dog's life!

Just look in the museum at the collars of the past.

There's a glittering collection that's spectacular and vast –

in the detail of the history from iron spikes to gold –

how dogs of poor and rich were treated in the days of old.

There are jewelled ones and heavy ones,

thin, and others thicker,

but the dog collar I'd like to choose is one to fit the vicar.

Castle wed

Castle wed in sky and water –

horizon joining man and wife.

The giving of a precious daughter –

marriage vows reflect through life.

Through the mazes, weaving rivers,

arms entwined at lover's lake.

Willows bow – revering shivers,

the joining cords that none may break.

Moat emotion hugs each corner,

tasting tears, embracing smiles.

Faithful, recording each performer

as our two white swans glide down the aisle.

Loveliest castle, loveliest bride,

loveliest day forever guide.

by Andrew Buller

The eye of the beholder

What beauty here in pureness lies

from every angle of her face

underneath the cloudless skies.

What beauty here in pureness lies?

Who can fail here to embrace

the timeless charm and sense of place?

What beauty here in pureness lies

from every angle of her face!

Reflect on this

Reflect on this. The earth has been turned
    upside-down
as I sit here upon this bank
    and reminisce.
How can my world so clean and bright
    so easily break down?
        Reflect on this.

Does memory disguise, conceal, bank thoughts,
    obscure the bliss
like visions of sweet chocolate, transformed
    to muddy brown
while clouds scud through the azure blue
    and then this scene dismiss?

The easel of my art is old and frail

    – like me – run-down –

but seeks to capture, like castle guards,

    anything amiss.

Reality recovers in a flash of wings

    – splashdown.

        Swans – reflect on this.

A rocky outcrop

A rocky outcrop in a stream
the jewelled watercourse it seems
can conjure any young man's dream
of future bliss devoid of screams.

The jewelled watercourse it seems
holds secrets deep inside its heart
of future bliss devoid of screams.
How soon will innocence depart?

Held secrets deep inside its heart
reflects the castle still to keep
how innocence will soon depart
when age's wolves attack the sheep.

Reflects the castle still to keep
a timeless truth – all will be well
when age's wolves attack the sheep,
bewitched, entranced, under the spell.

A timeless truth – all will be well –
can conjure any young man's dream
bewitched, entranced, under the spell
of rocky outcrop in a stream.

Playing around

Now I've been informed that I ought

to be more active – play some sport.

            I have thought. "Play I-Spy?

Surely that is good enough. Snap?

No? Not playing cards on my lap?

            Real sport?" I've got to try

golf. "On T.V.? Listen to talk?

What? Go outside and really walk?"

            It's all arranged – no argument –

I'm being taken off to Leeds

to play nine holes – my tear succeeds –

            nought – torture's imminent.

I stand and watch as others hit

whilst butterflies patrol my pit.

        My turn – breathe – gentle swings

and listen for the sweetest sound

of contact – ball the club has found –

        it sails – as birds on wings.

I'm asked when I return at last

if I've survived my cruel blast

        of exercise. I looked.

"You don't know what to me you've done!

Golf rounds at Leeds are so much fun

        I've joined the club. I'm hooked!"

Where sound Leeds

Hear the sound of trickling water,

calls of whoopers, gulls and geese,

laughter of the son and daughter

growing levels will increase.

Calls of whoopers, gulls and geese

mix into a raucous medley

growing levels will increase,

echoing across the bailey.

Mix into a raucous medley

one school party, then another

echoing across the bailey,

how that baby screams for mother.

One school party, then another

searching for the maze's end.

How that baby screams for mother.

Where's the peace? Just round the bend

searching for the maze's end.

Laughter of the son and daughter.

Where's the peace? Just round the bend –

hear the sound of trickling water.

The causeway leads

The solid causeway leads the eye

between security of walls,

above the pointed arches there

to let the moat flow freely through,

reflecting all who've trod this way before.

The cobbles are set firm and dry

so careful to avoid the falls

which gravity might me ensnare

into watery-arms – eschew

to join the hapless soldiers' long-gone war.

Standing and overshadowed, I

gaze heavenwards, through murder holes

(a gruesome name, but very fair)

where once poured boiling oil – it's true –

effective, but a practice we'd deplore.

Oaken doors, iron studs now try

to keep me out, like cannonballs

before, but open swung, declare

'step through – we're here to welcome you'

into the bailey, lawned, 'please do explore'.

Towers, ramparts, dominate sky

and mellowed sunlight gently calls

'further'. Does anything compare

with castle's majesty? It knew

I would be captured, always to adore.

Come walk with me

Come walk with me along the rampart's path

imagining those folk who in the past

have trod this way and viewed the moat – or cast

an enemy therein – unpleasant bath.

Descend to water's edge and feel the wrath

of victim from the brink – to hold him fast

and lead him, dripping, round the bend. At last

an open door – to find a welcome hearth?

Not yet. This Norman cellar's oh so cold

to keep the siege-food safe from spoils of war

with wine and ales in barrels, meat that's raw

and special store for candle wax and mould.

Uneven steps lead up to trip the old

who dare to gaze on armoured knight once more.

I have feelings

The instant that I felt the dawn

of life in me I was forlorn.

I felt uneasy in my skin

that very moment I was born.

> From underneath my wrinkled chin
>
> right down past chest to foot and shin
>
> I doubt myself that I will fit
>
> inside this carcass like a tin.

Rejection by a group will hit

my confidence. I'll have to quit.

Can't help the fact that I am new —

I'd like to fit in just a bit.

> At last, I feel within me grew
>
> a warmth — it feels so strange, but true.
>
> Inhabited within, blood flow
>
> spreads joy. I move — a life anew.

Adrenalin pumps to and fro

as to the heat of battle go

through raging fires and noise of war

my soul departs – a single blow.

    An empty shell in mud and gore

    on which the wind and rain will pour –

    I feel the chill of friendship gone.

    Will anything my warmth restore?

Yet now I stand the stair upon

and spiders with their cloaks they don

my suit – for centuries I've worn

stiff-lipped – an armour – still anon.

Upon the stair

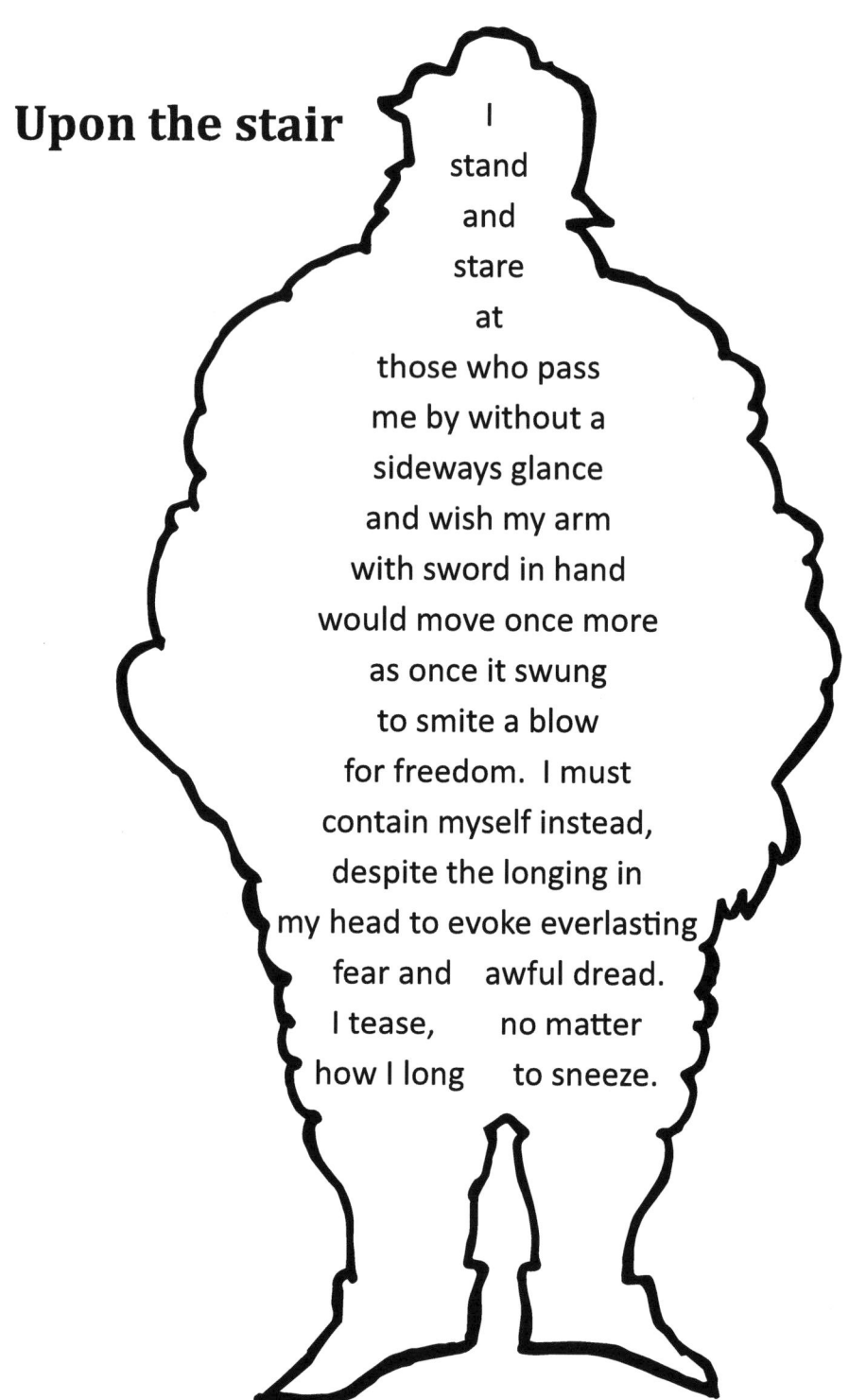

I stand and stare at those who pass me by without a sideways glance and wish my arm with sword in hand would move once more as once it swung to smite a blow for freedom. I must contain myself instead, despite the longing in my head to evoke everlasting fear and awful dread. I tease, no matter how I long to sneeze.

Rights

Piercing eyes look down

exuding power

their strength from certainty

their right to be here.

Long-gone they are

yet Thomas Fairfax

most of all

demands obedience.

Commander-in-Chief

of Parliamentary Army

led battles

to overthrow the Crown.

For civil dignity

and honesty renowned

refused to lead the judgement

of the King

because he knew it was

not right.

Queen's gallery

The light floods in

reflected by the waters down below

through wide-arched windows

to the solid oak beneath your feet.

How many souls

have trod this way before?

Designed for royal exercise

to walk

to pause for thought

admire the portraiture

the changing seasons mirrored in the moat.

Enjoy the gallery's delights

but forget not

Henry and his offspring

will see all

where light floods in.

The Queen's maidens

The Banqueting Hall, laid out in splendour,

the guests all in awe and filled with delight

under the gaze of His Royal Majesty,

servants all frantic, yet still – out of sight.

   Is this the place to natter

   where no platter's out of place?

   The finest table napkins

   have designs in Flemish lace.

   May I whisper to my sister

   or bring both of us disgrace?

   Our hostess's eyebrow twitch

   brings a redness to my face.

"Ladies. Be upstanding. The loyal toast!

To our beloved Catherine, tonight

we raise our cheer! We turn our back on husbands

– thus – and feast ourselves by candlelight!"

The dragon flies

The dragon flies

over the Field of the Cloth of Gold,

English King Henry

meeting Francis, the King of France,

each monarch

trying to impress the other

with vast retinues,

banquets and entertainments.

As night-time falls

excitement builds as each expects

the unexpected.

Flaming torches illuminate added dangers.

One bright spark

triggers the tethered touch-line

and races upwards,

exploding the arsenal of fireworks

hidden within

the belly of the dragon.

Pax vobiscum

As you enter a hush descends –
you have to pause – not pass on through –
"I must hurry," your mind contends,
"Pax vobiscum – Peace be with you."

History exudes from every wall.
Royals, nobles, have stood here too
as saints or sinners – welcomed all,
"Pax vobiscum – Peace be with you."

Glass-fronted, locked, the treasures lie,
safe from harm yet in full view
and wooden painted scenes all cry,
"Pax vobiscum – Peace be with you."

Drawn to stay, but must continue,
"Pax vobiscum – Peace be with you."
"I can't afford to miss my bus!"
"Pax nobiscum – Peace be with us."

The Kyrielle poetic form is based on the 'Kyrie Eleison – Lord have mercy upon us', a repeated call heard during the Mass.

May 22nd 1520

Picture the scene.

The Banqueting Hall prepared for the queen

and king on his way to travel to France –

a feast for the eyes, such great food, merry dance

to follow for any who offend or falter

which is why I am here, prostrate at the altar.

Such honour bestowed is not very nice –

five thousand for dinner exacts a huge price.

Twist

Round the twist?

You will be as you climb

yet do not rush.

Admire the craftsmanship

how light will play with shadows

but beware the birds and beasts

that lurk amidst the linen folds.

The single tree's trunk

to which each tread

is firmly fixed

takes you spiralling around

to reach stability

beside a laughing crusader.

Cool warmth

At the heart of the Gloriette, a hole,

brings welcome light.

The courtyard flagstones wear the tread of years,

yet secrets keep.

The fountain's rhythmic drips mark passing time,

without a pause

whilst sun-filled days, the warming sandstone walls

reflect the heat

enticing wistful glances through the glass

of passing eyes.

Simplicity of functional design,

a perfect place.

Lady Baillie

Lady Baillie, elegantly poised
in window, framed by moat and park,
comfortable in her home, her castle,
surrounded by her loves, her passions,
relaxed in her little country retreat,
welcoming guests from high society,
the world of films and royal households
yet shyly tending to her aviaries –
in short – enjoying her life to the full
and planning how to pass on her legacy
to her adopted nation.

Timepiece

S
  U
    N
      D
        I
          A
            L

seeks strong sunshine

sits serene – stoic solitude

sun's sweet shafts

send shadows

surreptitiously

shifting

stealing

seconds

swiftly

softly

suspiciously

seemingly sad – such silence

The new castle

The buildings to the bailey's north
demolished, made the way for Jacobean mansion
to create a modern feel of comfort.

Yet prisoners-of-war
lacked appreciation for their royal residence,
firing the Gloriette into disrepair.

Wealth from America and wives enabled updating,
yet fashionable taste for Strawberry Hill Gothic
meant tacking shapely boards across the windows.

Fiennes Wykeham Martin had the means
to rescue the perishing
and demolish the disfigured mansion.

The New Castle emerged swiftly.

along with the restored Gloriette.

Built to impress in the Tudor style –

it does.

Its welcome warmth shines through every stone.

The Maiden's Tower

King Richard the Second – four pence per day –
authorised payment be made to recluse,
Christina Hyde, alone in her cell to say
prayers for the souls who pass. Tudor use
grew for ladies-in-waiting – then mainstay
as brewhouse – workshop – luxurious flat.
Could a Conference Centre be better than that?

Let's face it

The years take their toll of trees.
Some succumb to lightning strikes –
others to disease.
The animals may nibble at the roots
or high in boughs
and frosts may cause the sap to freeze.
All these cause individualities.

None of them are commonplace.
Were damage made maliciously
would be a huge disgrace.
But this one's natural.
It's grown here in this space
and sports its own fox face.

In its waters

The shadows of their darkness slowly creep

over the warmed and glowing castle wall –

the stillness in its waters safely keep

secrets – hidden from those inside – asleep

to messages the clouds will bring for all.

The shadows of their darkness slowly creep.

Will vision safe returned – round corners peep –

etch in cipher's code a transient scrawl?

The stillness in its waters safely keep

more secrets in the moat that lies so deep –

still hidden, those who from the ramparts fall.

The shadows of their darkness slowly creep

and cry for retribution – will they weep?

Underneath ripples there's no waterfall –

the stillness in its waters safely keep

nine centuries of shadows, but their Keep

could tumble under force of cannonball.

The shadows of their darkness slowly creep

and stillness in its waters safely keep.

To sit and stare

To stroll and stare

at passing creatures on their way

to stroll and stare

or fly or swim where'er they dare

from their security to stray

without becoming simply prey.

To stroll and stare.

To stand and stare

to find a different point of view.

To stand and stare –

with further distance eyes can share

the vistas opening up, true blue

skies, lofty trees and green fields too.

To stand and stare.

To sit and stare

to capture each and every scene.

To sit and stare

without pressure, released from care

of our whirlwind life, pleasure glean

when take the time to marvel how serene.

To sit and stare.

Plantation

The hurricane of eighty-seven
    wreaked havoc here in Kent.
Things blew down and then took off
    and no-one knows just where they went.
Our woodland trees all suffered so.
At Leeds they planted, row on row,
a beech plantation, here to grow
    and shelter us with money,
well-spent!

Grandmother's treat

"Just sit there – still – yes – for a while – just pause.
This bench is here for us to use. So you –
you've played the princess rescued by the knight –
disappeared into the maze – out of sight –
and leaving me, not knowing what to do.
You found me – that was good – minus one shoe
so limped along – or hopped along – but right
it seemed to run for an ice cream – in spite
of all the agonies. I really knew
you were not hurt. – You gave your bag to who?
He told you it would be quite safe – alright –
I must retrace (my thoughts are impolite).
You think he wore a uniform – it's blue.
    Where's the switch to close this crocodile's jaws?"

A slant on history

With such a complex history, these poems try to capture the changing times through some of the colourful characters who have trodden these ways before us.

Leeds Castle has over nine hundred years of history and the ode, the ballad and the sestina forms of poetry offer greater scope to explore these stories.

Early days

From greensand ridge a spring does flow

to form the River Len below –

by Lenham village gently through the hay –

ten miles further on to join the Medway.

Every fresh water source

is highly prized, of course,

and fertile land beside it too

gave early man the food he grew

or hunted in the wooded slopes – and so

community was formed – right here – we know.

When the Norman William conquered,
partitioning of land occurred.
To Bishop Odo of Bayeux came Kent
and he his days in lavish lifestyle spent.
Wood for fire to keep warm
allowed people to form
stronger units. One called Lesledes
flourished, fulfilling all their needs
and based on river islands it is clear –
brought security – at least reduced the fear.

The Domesday Survey had a look
at every part and filled a book.
With mills along the River Len and more –
land owned and values – surprise – taxes soar –
but William's son, his heir,
Rufus, became aware –

Uncle Odo's behaviour bad

upset the king so he was glad

to gift Lesledes to Hamo de Crevecour

whose family lived here a century and more.

Hamo's grandson Robert, built of stone

an island Keep to call his own.

"Lower the drawbridge!" gave bailey access

where all domestic duties could progress.

(All of this was seen

in eleven-nineteen.)

Alas, King Henry had no son.

Daughter Matilda support won

from Crevecours, but nephew Stephen sought

to take the crown – it was his single thought.

He did. Boy was he cross? He sent

his army to lay siege, here in Kent.

The Crevecours steadfastly stayed inside

the Keep, there was no other place to hide.

The soldiers went away.

Common sense the best way

forward to resolve these disputes –

forgiveness – the family make roots.

The eleven-thirty-nine siege took place –

but castle proudly stood and saved its face.

Eleanor came at sweet thirteen

to be King Edward's royal Queen.

This Castille girl was especially clever

and acquired lands through debts and whenever

she could. Practice succeeds

to earn her Keep in Leeds.

In twelve-seventy-eight she made

decisions here to simply upgrade –

make Keep into a Gloriette – her treat –

and build up bailey's walls to thirty feet.

The ballad of Eleanor

Come peasants all and hear the tale

of Princess Eleanor

from Castile's lands, just twelve years old,

her story we'll explore.

    Marriage contracts fathers gained

    to bolster their prestige

    and so her hand was promised –

    to Edward owed her liege.

        In Burgos monastery they wed,

        twelve-fifty-four the date,

        though second-cousins-once-removed

        together sealed their fate.

            A foreigner for England bound –

            unpopular – spoke French.

            Weak children bore – almost recluse –

            till barons caused a stench.

Sweet Eleanor defied them all

held on to Windsor Castle

till Edward captured – almost gone –

but won the Evesham battle.

    The government was then reformed

    so confidence was blooming

    as Eleanor bore healthy fruit

    with credence swiftly growing.

        Still in her twenties, they set sail,

        a crusade then to lead.

        Beset by troubles, Edward stabbed,

        (not a good place to bleed).

            Returned to England, Henry dead

            so Edward now is King.

            It's time for Eleanor to see

            how far her power she'll fling.

Intelligent, and ruthless too,

from debts she gathered land.

Her mind was clear, she took control,

her every moved was planned.

    And so to Kent the queen then came

    to survey her estate

    of Leeds with moated castle Keep

    and fertile lands – "That's great!"

        Her builders built and modernised

        for comfort from the wet

        surrounding waters there then rose

        the glorious Gloriette.

            Knives with handles, even forks,

            expensive luxuries

            with tableware and carpets too

            and walls with tapestries.

This ballad ends as this tale must

in Eleanor's demise.

Thirty-six years a loyal bride –

no wonder Edward cries.

    From Lincoln back to London Town

    her coffin safely rested.

    Each night well-guarded, where she lay,

    Edward then invested

        a monument to stand through time

        to signify his loss

        at every stopping place to find

        an Eleanor Cross.

The most famous of these crosses stands outside Charing Cross Station.

The young queens

In 1290 Queen Eleanor sadly died. The king decreed that where

her coffin lay overnight a cross be built. From Lincolnshire to

London, thirteen resting places were to be seen –

Charing Cross the final stop. King Edward mourned for

nine whole years until he found the right

Princess in France, 17-year-old Margaret, to reign by his side.

A dowry gift to his new bride – there to reside

in tranquillity – Leeds Castle – somewhere

for her – for life. He also agreed her niece would be right

to wed his son and so it was that Edward Two

in 1308, married Isabella – renowned for

beauty and intelligence at 12. Their marriage problems were

unforeseen.

Edward relied on confidantes. If Isabella caused a scene –

he'd take their side –

he gave very little for

his young queen to do. They lost a battle with the Scots where

both were nearly captured and, in 1312, the barons turned too.

Civil war began outright.

Defeat at Bannockburn, a famine – what was going right?

Two sons were born and French help was seen

as the only way to

win, but Isabella was alone – beside

herself with cares. A pilgrimage to Canterbury, but where

to stay on the way? Leeds Castle she'd heard of before.

In 1321 Baroness Badlesmere refused admission, therefore

a fight began, but later siege turned out alright

for victory restored some royal power throughout the
countryside.

Reprisals were cruelly obscene.

Defeat again by Scots – abandoned Isabella aware

that Edward and she were at an end too.

By 1326 with her lands and children taken, hitherto

loyal Isabella found allies in France and seized power for

herself as Regent. Edward abdicated. The country sighed,

peace but lasted till Edward Three claimed his birthright

and Isabella faded from power, but rose in wealth, seen

through lands acquired everywhere.

Leeds Castle too saw this history put right

for finally returned to Queen – overseen

by waterside – till 1358. Usurpers beware!

The seasons

Leeds Castle and its estate change with the seasons and the weather. A passing cloud creates a shadow, a chill, a touch of fear and yet foreboding melts away as warm glows return.

A royal spring

The heralds of the season play their part

with snowdrops proudly holding high their face

above the chilling earth, proclaiming art

in virgin white, serene, proud of their place –

    right here.

Court jesters next take centre stage in gold,

with purple flowing raiments or of creams

whilst singing, shouting messages so bold

relate their tales that focus all our dreams –

    dispel the fear.

The pikemen come. They brandish high their spears

so green, stand stiff, aloof, until crack will

from armoured sheath reveal, at last, their ears

and glorious heads, so nods each daffodil –

    and thus to all give cheer.

A multitude of flora bursts to life

to triumph over winter's failing hand.

The court is filled with splendour where the wife

of king's the same as any in the land –

    why cherish castle grounds is clear!

"Let mists arise!"

"Let mists arise!"

a single shaft of sunlight cries.

That slender slip of light is all it takes

to stir the surface of the lakes

to shroud our view

and bid the distant past adieu –

cloak vision swift in mystery

and change the shape of history.

It's hot!

Leeds' gates opening – car parks are filling
    their slot
Mums sunblock spreading – it's an exciting
    fleshpot
stewards marshalling – wristband issuing
    it's hot!

hands sanitising – keenly entering
    the plot
paths meandering – footsteps echoing
    gunshot
mallards are quacking – tufted ducks diving
    a lot

mighty trees shading – great chainsaw carving
 their knot
waterfalls tumbling – lazy fish swimming
 or not
children tree climbing – jumping and running
 somewhat

parents wandering – toddlers escaping
 they trot
ice creams awaiting – cool lollies licking
 hotspot
coffee cups frothing – drink sales rocketing
 teapot

liquid refreshing – wildlife abounding
    nice spot
portcullis guarding – mighty walls rising
    pot-shot
castle imposing – water surrounding
    snapshot

vision reflecting – snappers reviewing
    great shot
return slopes coming – temperatures rising
    where squat
pensioners puffing – bench seat beckoning
    it's hot!

The leaves are turning

The leaves are turning. Spring's glorious greens

are memories. They'd burst our painted scenes

of winter browns, the greys and chilly ice

that lied that nature's dead. Longer days means

sunshine's powers will win over the vice –

like grip of arctic winds. Then in a trice

the blossom breaks out. Insects gathering

nectar become themselves a sacrifice

to birds, so intent on multiplying,

victims of food chains, so satisfying

the needs of predators. Through summertime

leaves are turning, chlorophyll sweetening

sap that's rising, sugars storing, sublime

in growth held high, aloft above the grime

of earth and human folly. Trees have stood

here, resplendent for decades, in their prime.

But the leaves are turning. The likelihood

that winds will strip them soon, misunderstood

by some as gloom. They're not evergreens.

The rest is needed to protect our wood.

The English autumn

The English autumn season heralds change

from lingering summer's sun and gentle breeze

to chilly nights and winds that disarrange

the twigs and rustic leaves on all the trees

so we might yearn, or look back with regret

from lingering summer's sun and gentle breeze.

We walk on grass where blades now drip with sweat

and wonder why such simple pleasures lie

so we might yearn or look back with regret

if we ignore and simply pass on by.

Lift up your gaze, observe the subtle shades

and wonder why such simple pleasures lie

in colours soft yet vibrant to our eyes.

The more you stare, the more you will approve.

Lift up your gaze, observe the subtle shades.

So don a thicker coat, don't disapprove.

The more you stare, the more you will approve.

The English autumn season heralds change

to chilly nights and winds that disarrange.

Foggy Leeds

Engulfed by fog my eyes cannot believe –
everything distorted – there are no skies –
the weeping willows find their thin disguise
as mighty oaks fools only the naïve.
The fluttering of wings the ears deceive
as ghostly flights of fear my mind applies –
     engulfed by fog.

Appearing from the gloom my eyes perceive
a solid mass – discarding its disguise –
rising majestically – defying spies –
reflecting as if only make-believe –
     engulfed by fog.

Christmas trees

The castle was with Christmas trees bedecked
    for all to gaze at marvellous beauty,
    bringing such joy, sparkling resplendently,
displayed in every room to great effect.
Beside great mirrors, there to help reflect
    upon the twinkling stars of light, brightly
    shining hope towards the fireplace chimney
where children's wishes hopefully expect.
    Twenty-twenty then gloom instead has spread.
    Leeds Castle staff must seek to find a plan.
Be artistic, wood, fabric and plastic,
    make modern designs housed in a shed,
    music of carols wafting through trees, can
delight and intrigue. They have. Fantastic!

Winter colours

What colours will my visit bring this day?
From cheerful wristband signal that we've paid
to purest snowdrop white that proudly states,
'I'm here!' though winter's icy chill dictates
that we brave souls should in our homes have stayed
    instead of seeking pleasures here today.

Has Aragon from slumber raised her head
or long, bronzed tail unfurled to snare a child?
Hiding amongst the canes of green bamboo
she watches, one eye closed, at what you do,
red-hatted, purple coated, single filed,
    avoiding crowds, yet seeking crocus bed.

Your head is raised to seek the heavenly blue

amidst the greys of mists that swallow land

to spy the flash of iridescent hues

of kingfisher, a moment's passing views

across the flooded field, we understand

        that chocolate mud will stick to us like glue.

The black path winds amongst the trees so old

and mallard drakes proclaim their bold intent

to ward off challengers for their mate's love

whilst subtle shades bedeck the collared dove

nestled safely, warmed by sun's rays sent

        to turn the castle walls to glowing gold.

Years to remember

2020 was a year like no other. From glorious displays of decorated trees throughout the castle, to total closure for months, partial opening and rules to follow, lifted and re-imposed. Such an inspirational Christmas tree display in a succession of garden sheds gave us cheer at the year's end. 2021 followed in similar vein, with restrictions, cautious optimism, doubts and summer sunshine bringing in the crowds, especially when booking was no longer required.

Throughout the staff have performed magnificently and these few poems are a reminder that, despite any difficulty, you will always receive the warmest welcome at Leeds Castle.

Released from lockdown's grip

At ten o'clock the mighty gates swing wide

and in our safe, tin-boxes we all ride,

our pass displayed so we are waved on through,

following, yet not knowing what to do.

We park and cross to portacabin hut

where tickets checked, I do feel like a nut.

"Which is the sticky end ('cos I can't see)

to turn this strip to round identity?"

Now wash and sanitize here at the station

(just as we've all been trained throughout the nation).

The tarmac pathway here, clearly defines –

keep your social distance – follow the signs.

Relax – and breath – between the shrubs and trees.

Ignore precipitation in the breeze.

The mute swans glide serenely on the lake

whilst mallard hen is pestered by her drake.

The winding pathway gives us history

on sunken plaques with dates for all to see.

Around each curve more treasures are in view –

a sculptured swan – carved to form a pew

to rest upon and watch the world go by

or simply marvel at the changing sky.

Stare instead at the sheer scale of gunnera,

catching rain in upturned leaf-like umbrella.

The birds are still, but gentle streams bring sounds
throughout the journey through the peaceful grounds.
Emerging up a slope I find a lake
and pause awhile the vista to intake.
Beyond the swooping martins, ducks and geese
I spy a wooden fortress to release
energetic children's armies, fighting their
imaginary foes, whilst parents find a chair.

Majestic, in its moat of polished glass,
the castle sits, surrounded by its grass-
covered bank and mighty walls of stone –
towering – aloof, "I'm here alone."
The single entrance route is shut quite fast.
No-one enters here till danger's past.
So turn around, escape just while you may
and live and learn to come another day.

We do, but pause to watch a little child

delighted to see birds so free and wild.

Such simple pleasures, innocence of youth,

oblivious to panic, only truth

of love and comfort in grandmother's arms,

keeping her happy, free from worldly harms.

Our first release from lockdown truly succeeds

to lift our spirits – here in Kent's own Leeds.

Set benchmarks high

At Leeds, the Castle staff set benchmarks high
for quality of service everywhere
and since the lockdown eased, with law comply
yet keep the welcome warm, alert, aware
of every guest. Each one has special needs –
for tranquil paths beside the water's edge
or watching wagtails forage near the reeds –
or play a knight on bended knee to pledge
allegiance to the crown, to fight the foe –
and rescue, maybe, damsels in distress –
until his mother says it's time to go.
The signs are there, stay safe, gently progress
along the paths beside the moat and views
to savour all that Leeds Castle values.

Golfers' roundelay

Golfers must delay their round –

lockdown measures are in force.

Rumours when they'll start, abound –

stirring talk of quick divorce –

for patience some are not renowned,

but everyone must wait off course.

Rumours when they'll start, abound –

stirring talk of quick divorce.

News at last for those who're browned

daylight comes – precious resource

for patience some are not renowned,

but everyone must wait off course.

News at last for those who're browned

daylight comes – precious resource.

On the tee – the battleground

stretches out though feeling coarse

for patience some are not renowned,

but everyone must wait, of course.

On the tee – the battleground

stretches out though feeling coarse

hit the trees – beware rebound –

try your best – avoid the gorse

for patience some are not renowned,

but everyone must wait, of course.

Hit the trees – beware rebound –
try your best – avoid the gorse –
pause – and take a look around –
castle in its watercourse.
For patience some are not renowned,
but everyone must wait, of course.

Pause – and take a look around –
castle in its watercourse –
adults enjoy your own playground,
the company and good discourse
for patience some are not renowned,
but everyone must wait, of course.

Adults enjoy your own playground,

the company and good discourse

your round complete – victor crowned –

who thanks you for your candid sauce.

For patience some are not renowned,

but everyone must wait – or curse.

Leeds Castle

"The loveliest castle in the world"

Printed in Great Britain
by Amazon